RAISING UP
REPLANTERS

Available in the Replant Series

RAISING UP REPLANTERS

MARK HALLOCK

 ACOMA PRESS

To all the pastors and churches that desire to be part of the replanting movement. Thank you for taking a leap of faith, trusting God, and investing in the replanters who will lead this movement, by the grace and power of God. The Lord is glorified in you!

CONTENTS

FORWARD

One of the great joys in life and in ministry can be found in raising up leaders to carry on the mission of Jesus through proclaiming the gospel and building the church. One of the biggest challenges we face is in figuring out how to fulfill this important task--especially if you serve a normative (a congregation under 299) size church.

With churches closing at a rate of close to 900 a year we find ourselves at a critical crossroads. We must raise up men who are called, qualified and trained to be competent to pastor in the towns, cities, and churches that are often overlooked. Churches who once thrived in proclaiming the Gospel and reaching their communities now find themselves in a fight for survival, often having little hope that a pastor would be willing to come and shepherd them toward their future.

Ministry training programs and residencies are commonly found in larger and more innovative churches. Their trainees benefit from their learning experiences but often focus more of their learning on the administration and philosophy of ministry rather than actually engaging deeply in all facets of ministry.

In training at a normative size church a Pastoral Resident will likely get more experience preaching to a congregation rather than his classmates. He will get one on one focused time with the Lead Pastor and Elders or Deacons. He will be encouraged to form relationships inter-generationally rather than sticking with his own demographic. He can propose, plan and execute ministry projects and be coached and encouraged along the way. He strengths can be affirmed and developed and his weaknesses can be known and addressed.

Who better to raise up replanters than those who are actively engaged in the work of replanting themselves?

Pastoral demands are great, sermons don't write themselves, congregants need care and the everyday administration of ministry can't be handed off and forgotten. The days and the weeks roll on, becoming years, and well intentioned thoughts of developing leaders to not only share the ministry but to be sent and mobilized for ministries of their own becomes a dream that's never realized.

It doesn't have to be that way.

In the pages that follow you'll find a theologically sound, relationally rich and easily executable plan for raising up and equipping men whom God can and will use to bring hope and help to struggling churches. The Calvary Family of Churches and their Lead Pastor, Mark Hallock are co-laborers in the work of replanting, they know from experience just how difficult and how wonderful the work of reviving a dying church can be. I've seen first-hand the fruit of Calvary's residency process and I'm convinced that a church of any size can raise up leaders using this plan.

My prayer is that God would call you to let go of whatever it is that is holding you back from calling and equipping men for the important work of replanting.

Replant for the Glory of God and the Good of the Community,

Bob Bickford
Associate Director of Replant
North American Mission Board

RAISING UP REPLANTERS

Leaders. We need them. Big time.

Strong, humble, visionary yet convictional leaders can be tough to find in the church these days. And yet the need for these types of leaders is greater than ever. This is particularly true when it comes to helping replant and revitalize dying churches. As we watch record numbers of congregations closing their doors each and every week all across our country, we are constantly reminded of the leadership crisis in which we find ourselves. We need pastors who can lead healthy change in a declining church with passionate vision and a shepherd's heart. The question is: Where do we find them?

Ministry leadership coach, Brian Howard, writes,

> Are you hoping that ready-made leaders will show up to help you lead the church? Are you trusting seminaries or other churches to raise up leaders for your church? If so, you will likely be waiting a long time. There are simply not enough ready-made leaders to do what we need to do in ministry.[1]

Howard is right. Every church has a responsibility to strategically identify, develop, and deploy leaders of various kinds in numerous areas of ministry. This is especially true when it comes to the development of church replanters. Local churches must take seriously their call and responsibility to identify, equip and send replanters out to lead and shepherd dying churches.

For too long the church has assumed this kind of intentional leadership development is primarily the role and responsibility of our seminaries. But this is wrong. Our seminaries serve a vital role in the education of those in various forms of vocational ministry. However, our seminaries do not take the place of the local church. The local church is, and always has been, the primary environment for the development of pastors and church leaders. Al Mohler, President of The Southern Baptist Theological Seminary puts it well when he writes,

> The role of theological seminaries remains crucial for the education and training of Christian ministers. At its best, the seminary is an intentional gathering of Christian scholars who are dedicated to the preparation of ministers, committed to biblical truth, gifted in modeling and teaching the tasks of ministry, and passionate about the Gospel... Nevertheless, count me as one seminary president who believes that the local church is even more important to the education of the pastor. The local church should see theological education as its own responsibility before it partners with a theological seminary for concentrated studies. The seminary can provide a depth and breadth of formal studies — all needed by the minister — but it cannot replace the local church as the context where ministry is learned most directly.[2]

Of course, the question is, what does this look like practically? How can churches be directly involved in the development of pastors and church leaders? For our purposes, what does it look like for a local church to prepare and equip a replanter for the ministry of church revitalization? I believe one answer to these questions is through the development of a replanting residency in your congregation.

WHAT IS A REPLANTING RESIDENCY?

When many people hear the word "Residency," they immediately think of terms like "Residency Program" or "Resident," often associated with the medical community. Those individuals serving as medical residents are often already on a trajectory toward becoming doctors, nurses, or other types of health care providers. However, they spend their "residency" learning from and shadowing more experienced doctors and nurses, while practicing medicine in an environment where they can experience honest feedback, mentoring, and learning. In a similar way, a replanting residency helps to create an environment where potential church replanters are able to learn from more seasoned pastors and leaders, get needed ministry experience in the context of a local church, and they get do it all in a safe and secure environment designed to help them grow as ministers of the Gospel.

Now you might be wondering why your church should consider starting a replanting residency program. Perhaps you can understand the need for churches to create residencies that help equip future church replanters, but why should your church be one of these? Why should your congregation begin a replanting residency program? That's a great question. Let me give you some reasons to consider.

TEN REASONS TO START A RESIDENCY

Reason #1: It's biblical.

To be a biblical church is to be a developer of leaders. We see this throughout Scripture. Ephesians 4:12, among other places, is clear that the local church is called to "equip the saints for the work of ministry, for building up the body of Christ." We see throughout the ministry of Jesus that he poured into his disciples, leading them, teaching them, preparing them for ministry themselves. In his relationship with Timothy, we observe the Apostle Paul investing in a young pastor, equipping him and then sending him out to preach the Gospel and lead God's people. If we are to be biblical churches, we must seek to be congregations that intentionally raise up pastors and deploy them into the harvest. A replanting residency can help your church do this.

Reason #2. Any size church can do it!

I have run into pastors and church members who think only large churches can do something like this. Only large churches have the resources to pull off doing a residency program that develops replanters. This is simply not true. In fact, I would say, often times the best replanting residencies happen in smaller churches. Smaller congregations are where a replanter can get an incredible amount of experience doing a variety of things, working with a variety of people from different backgrounds and ages on a personal, relational level. Whether your church is large, medium, or small, you can do this! You have all the resources you need to train up and send out a replanter from your congregation.

Reason #3. Churches help each other.

It is such a sweet thing to see churches work together in unity. We know this is something that is close to the heart of Jesus. In John 17:21, Jesus prays words that are true not just for individual Christians but for congregations. He prays, "That they may all be one, just as you, Father, are in me, and I in you, that they also may be in us, so that the world may believe that you have sent me." One of the many ways we can display this type of God-honoring unity is through churches helping one another; sharing resources, giving encouragement, serving one another in tangible ways, whatever it might look like, the Lord is honored when churches cooperate and each other. We are always better together!

When it comes to replanting, what a joy it is for a church that has raised up a replanter to send him out to love and lead a declining congregation in need of help. Moreover, there is joy for the individuals who are part of the sending church to come alongside the revitalizing congregation for the long haul, helping them to experience fresh life and vitality in the Lord. It is a good thing when churches help one another like this. We are all part of the same body of Christ. We all have the same Holy Spirit within us. We have all been given the same mission to proclaim the Gospel and make disciples of all nations for the glory of God. A replanting residency allows your church to help a struggling church as you intentionally seek to prepare their future pastor to lead them and serve them with the love of Christ.

Reason #4: Your church could use some help from a replanting resident.

Of course, while a replanting residency is designed to equip and prepare a replanter to go out and revitalize a dying congregation, until they are sent out, your church will benefit greatly from his service in your congregation. Having another pastor in training to help teach Sunday school classes, preach in the weekend worship gatherings, help with children's and youth ministry, do pastoral visits, as well as other duties in the church, is a huge blessing to the leadership and congregation.

Reason #5: Seeing replanting pastors thrive in their God-given gifts and passions is a delight.

One of the great joys in church replanting is to see a replanter come alive as they use the gifts and lean into the passions God has given them for ministry. Developing replanters should be seen as both a privilege and joy for any congregation.

Reason #6: Your church needs to be stretched.

One of the great benefits in starting a replanting residency is that it stretches your congregation. Replanters may or may not have a family, but if they do have a family, a replanting residency stretches your people to invest in, help encourage, and equip not only this replanter, but his wife and children as well. Sadly, many of our churches are stagnant. Many of our churches are stuck in our comfort zones and predictable routines. A big reason for this, in my opinion, is that our churches are not intentionally seeking to develop leaders. A replanting residency forces your people to catch a vision for leadership development and to play a role in the purposeful equipping of a future replanting pastor. This kind of stretching is a good thing for your people. They need it whether they realize it or not. This type of residency will help grow your people and give them a larger vision for the Kingdom.

Reason #7: The need for church replanting and revitalization is massive.

Perhaps this point is obvious, but it needs to be stated again. With large numbers of churches throughout our country closing their doors for the final time each and every week, there has never been a need for trained replanters more than there is today. Where are these replanters going to come from? The church down the street? The megachurches in your denomination? If we all take this attitude, very few replanters will ever be developed and sent out. We need a movement of churches that are passionate about equipping and sending replanting pastors out of their congregation. Churches plant churches. Churches also *replant* churches. If we are going to see a movement of replanting in our country and around the world, it will start with churches like yours that get into the game. To help your congregation get into the game of replanting, creating a replanting residency is a great place to start.

Reason #8: We care about reaching those far from God.

Every one of our communities is filled with people who are far from God. They do not know Jesus as their Lord and Savior. They have never heard the true Gospel of grace. The question is: who is going to proclaim this Gospel to them if not Christians in local churches within our communities? Yes, we must plant new churches. But we must also replant dying churches. Countless neighborhoods in cities and towns all over our country will be most effectively reached through revitalized churches in that community... churches that have been declining for years... churches that have become ineffective in bringing health and transformation to the community. If we care about reaching the lost, we will care about replanting churches. And if we care about replanting churches, we will care about equipping replanting pastors who will lead those churches to reach the lost, the hurting, and the broken that surround them.

Reason #9: The local church is the best place to train pastors.

As mentioned above, while I am so thankful for our seminaries, seminary is not designed to raise up and send out pastors and replanters. Local churches do this. Seminaries educate and sharpen. This is a great thing. It is essential for healthy, biblical leadership in the church. We need more of it. However, local churches primarily coach, train and mentor. Churches observe the life of a future pastor. A local church is the place where gifts are recognized, affirmed and nurtured. The local church is called to this, not seminary.

Reason #10. It's fun!

You read that correctly. It is fun! It is fun to be part of God's work in calling, equipping, and sending a replanter and his family out to serve a dying church. It is fun to have a passionate, mission-minded replanter around your church. If the replanter is married with children, it is fun to have his wife and children be part of your congregation for a season. There is much joy in doing this type of ministry together as a church. And ministry should be joyful! Ministry should not be a burden but a delight! I truly believe that starting a replanting residency in your congregation will spark fresh joy, vision, and excitement about God and what He can do in and through your church family for His glory.

THREE QUESTIONS FOR DEVELOPING A RESIDENCY

Once your church has decided to move forward in starting a replanting residency, what is next? Good question. There are three foundational questions that will guide you in this. These questions are:

1. What are we looking for in a replanting resident?
2. What do we want to develop in the replanting resident?
3. How do we train and prepare him to replant a church?

These three questions will help tremendously as you seek clarity on what you want the replanting residency to look like. Let's start with the first question, which gets at the heart of the kind of resident you desire to bring on.

What are we looking for in a replanting resident?

The first step in this process is becoming crystal clear on what exactly you are looking for in a potential replanting resident. There are several non-negotiables you are looking for in this individual. Here are five of them:

Mark #1: Passion and Hunger for God and His Word

We desperately need leaders in the church who are first and foremost passionate about God and his Word. A pastor cannot give to others what he does not own himself. The first thing you are looking for in a potential replanting resident is a deep love for God and his Word. You want to hear how he came to know Christ as Savior and Lord. You want to listen for ways in which he seeks to commune with God in worship and prayer. Is he passionate about Christ and the Gospel? Does he seek to love God and honor Him with his whole heart? What about his relationship with the Bible? You want to hear his view of Scripture. You want to know without a shadow of a doubt that he is absolutely committed to the inspiration, authority, and sufficiency of the Bible. However, more than simply his stated doctrinal convictions, you want to hear of his own personal love and hunger for God's Word. Does He love God and love God's Word? This is foundational and absolutely essential.

Mark #2: Deep Love and Care for People

Ministry is all about people. Replanting a dying church is all about loving and caring for people. In fact, there is no way to replant a dying church in a healthy, biblical, God-honoring way apart from a deep love and care for the people in that congregation. When you are looking for a replanting resident, you need to make sure, as best you can, that they love people. They don't just put up with people, they love people! They enjoy people. They encourage people. They serve people. They hug people. They love people! If this characteristic is not present in a potential replanting resident, keep looking until you find a man who is marked by this kind of love for others. Jesus loves people. And He calls every replanting pastor to follow his lead in sacrificially and joyfully loving others as well.

Mark #3: Humble, Servant Heart

A heart of humility is a non-negotiable when looking for a replanting resident. What does this look like? Is this individual eager and joyful about doing the tasks no one else wants to do? Do they prefer being unnoticed for their service and good deeds rather than being noticed and praised by others for them? This is a significant indicator of what is going on in his heart. True humility before God and people is crucial, not only when serving as a resident, but when serving as a replanting pastor in a local church.

Mark #4: Hard Worker

Pastoral ministry is hard work. It is hard work that takes much sacrifice, physically, spiritually, and emotionally. If a replanting resident is lazy or is constantly making excuses versus faithfully and joyfully working "as unto the Lord," not only will this create tension among other leaders, but the congregation as a whole will lose respect for him. As a result, they won't follow his leadership. A potential replanting resident must count the cost of ministry leadership and be willing to work hard for the glory of God and the good of the church. If he is unwilling to work hard as a resident in your church, there is no reason to believe he will work any harder as a replanting pastor when you send him out from your church. The last thing a declining church needs is a lazy pastor. And the last thing your church needs is a lazy resident. It sounds harsh, but it is the truth.

Mark #5: Team Player Who Encourages Others

You want to find a team player. You want to find a resident who is not a Lone Ranger. Is this individual aligned with the vision, mission, doctrine, and values of your church? Does he seek to humbly work alongside others? Does he encourage others or does he see them as a threat of some kind? Does he have a posture of teachability or a "know it all" mentality? Your church is a family and the leaders, including this potential resident, must work as a team and lead as a team. A fun, loving, encouraging, humble, hard-working, team-minded lover of Jesus and people is the kind of individual you want to bring on as a replanting resident. Pray hard that God would send a man marked by these five characteristics. And continue to lift him up in prayer as he lives into this call as replanting resident.

What do we want to develop in the resident?

Once we find a replanting resident that is marked by these five characteristics, the next question is, what do we want to develop in this individual? In other words, how do you want to help him grow? What specific areas do you want to help him focus on and mature in as he prepares to replant a dying church? You must be clear on this. As the saying goes, "If you aim at nothing, you will hit it every time." This is especially true when it comes to residencies in the local church. We must be crystal clear on what we are shooting for. There are three areas that you want to focus on:

- The Head
- The Heart
- The Hands

The Head. The head deals with how the resident is growing in their thinking, in their mind, in their intellect, and in their biblical and doctrinal formulation. Are they growing theologically? Are they growing in their understanding of biblical shepherding and leadership? Are they growing in their understanding of what it means and looks like to multiply themselves and others as disciple-makers? Are they growing in their "head" understanding of both relational and emotional intelligence? Each of these areas, along with many others, focus on helping the resident grow intellectually. Another component of the "head" is helping the resident mature in conviction. In their time with your church, the replanting resident should develop greater biblical and theological conviction that will be critical once they are serving as the replanting pastor of a local congregation.

The Heart. How are you going to help this resident grow in their heart? In other words, their character. I would say there are two primary areas to focus on: humility and love. Are we helping this resident grow as a humble leader who genuinely loves people? Who cares for people really well? Who recognizes that this is the Lord's work and it's a joy and privilege to be a part of it? If a resident has incredible *head* knowledge but lacks a *heart* of humility and love, he will never make it as a church replanter. You must intentionally help him honestly evaluate and intentionally grow, by God's grace, in Christ-like humility and love. For this to happen, you must help the resident to be increasingly shaped by the daily application of the Gospel to every aspect of his life and ministry. This means encouraging his growth in daily, dependent, prayerful intimacy with Christ.

The Hands. "The hands" deal with skills and competency. This is the practical, equipping of a resident, helping him grow in ministry practice. There are many different areas of ministry skill where your resident will need to grow. These include: leadership strategy, preaching ability, pastoral visitation, handling conflict, leading a small group, connecting with individuals across generations, and many others. Your church is the perfect environment to help this resident gain hands-on ministry experience in these different areas. You will be blessed by having a leader like this serving in these various roles, and he will be blessed as he becomes more confident as a servant-leader in the church.

As you consider what you want to develop in your replanting resident, the Head, the Heart, and the Hands are critical. The resident needs to grow in each of these as he prepares to replant a dying church. It is a joy to come alongside a resident, helping them to mature by the grace of God and the power of the Spirit. Of course, the next question that naturally arises then is: How do we train him in these different ministry areas?

How do we train and prepare a replanting resident to replant a church?

This question gets to the nuts and bolts of what this residency is actually going to look like in your church. The replanting residency you will be creating should be designed to help replanting residents do three things: be **equipped** for effective replanting ministry, **explore** their vocational calling, and **engage** in practical ministry and leadership. Ideally, the residency should be a nine-to-twelve month program. While you may decide your residency will be longer or shorter in length, nine to twelve months has proven in many churches to be a duration that is appropriate and doable for the replanter. Beginning the residency in September and ending in August of the following year is, in many cases, a great timeframe to consider. January through December can also be an effective timeline. Let's consider the three main components of the residency in greater depth.

RESIDENCY COMPONENT #1: EQUIP

Equipping the replanter for future ministry is a key aspect to this residency. What exactly will this equipping look like? While your church may desire to include other elements, I would recommend your residency consist of three distinct learning environments: The Church Replanting Cohort, the Pastoral Cohort, and the Preaching Cohort.

The Church Replanting Cohort

This cohort will meet twice a month and will include the replanting resident, the pastor or pastors, other leaders in the church, and even other pastors, church leaders, replanters or potential replanters in the community that you would like to invite.[3] This learning environment is where most of the teaching designed to equip the resident specifically for leading a church replant back to health will be accomplished. There will be several books read each semester as part of this cohort experience, however, the bulk of the teaching will happen not through reading books, but through 40 specific teachings related to church replanting and revitalization. The teaching for this cohort breaks down like this:

40 Foundations of Biblical Revitalization

PART 1: Preparing for Biblical Revitalization (September – October)

1. What is Church Revitalization?
2. Why is Church Revitalization Needed?
3. Understanding God's Heart for Revitalization
4. Counting the Cost: Potential Disadvantages and Challenges in Revitalization
5. Counting the Joy: Potential Advantages and Opportunities in Church Revitalization
6. Is this Church Ready for Revitalization?
7. Am I Ready for Revitalization?

PART 2: The Heart of Biblical Revitalization (November – December)

8. Heart Posture #1: Humility
9. Heart Posture #2: Love
10. Heart Posture #3: Patience
11. Heart Posture #4: Faith
12. Heart Posture #5: Passion
13. Heart Posture #6: Joy

PART 3: The Priorities of Biblical Revitalization (January – March)

14. Humble, Dependent Prayer
15. The Power and Necessity of Shepherd Preaching

PART 5: Persevering in Biblical Revitalization (June-August)

32. Rooting Your Life and Ministry in the Gospel
33. Cultivating a Heart for Long Haul Ministry
34. Putting Your Marriage and Family First
35. Growing in Emotional Intelligence
36. Facing Criticism in a Godly Manner
37. Handling Conflict Biblically
38. Caring for Your Soul through Spiritual Disciplines
39. Managing Your Schedule
40. Training Up and Sending Out Church Revitalizers and Replanters

You will have the option to have your pastor teach on the "40 Foundations" or you can use our free video curriculum that covers these teachings. All you need for this Replant Cohort, including teacher and student notes, discussion questions, and the video and audio teachings of each lesson, are available and free for your use at *nonignorable.org* or *churchreplanters.com*.

While you may decide to follow a different format for your gathering, here is a basic meeting schedule you could use for a bi-weekly, two-hour meeting covering two of the foundations:

Replant Cohort Meeting Schedule

(2 hours, bi-weekly)

- **Opening & Session Overview (5 minutes):** Welcome, housekeeping items, open in prayer.

- **Instruction (25-30 minutes):** Watch the teaching video of the first Foundation for this session. If the cohort leader would rather teach the Foundation themselves (i.e. no video) they can use the teacher's notes during this time.

- **Discuss & Develop (20 minutes):** Guide cohort through discussion questions and exercises to stimulate thinking and work toward application.

- **Break (5 minutes)**

- **Instruction (25-30 minutes):** Watch the teaching video of the second Foundation for this session. Again, if the cohort leader would rather teach the Foundation without the video, they can use the teacher's notes during this time.

- **Discuss & Develop (20 minutes):** Guide cohort through discussion questions and exercises to stimulate thinking and work toward application.

- **Wrap Up (10 minutes):** Review the key insights of this session and announce any assignments for the next gathering, pray and dismiss.

The Pastoral Cohort

Once a month the replanting resident will meet with your pastor and other leaders in your church for the purpose of learning about and growing in pastoral shepherding ministry. This cohort takes place in a roundtable discussion format and will study a book of your choice each semester that focuses on pastoral shepherding ministry. This book will help facilitate conversation and in-depth discussion around matters pertaining to pastoral ministry such as: knowing, leading, feeding, and protecting God's people in the local church.[4]

The Preaching Cohort

The preaching cohort is designed to help the replanting resident grow as a communicator of God's Word. One of the key ingredients to healthy, biblical revitalization is strong preaching of the Word each and every week. God works powerfully through His Word in the hearts of his people. The Spirit uses the Word of God to bring dead churches back to life, just as He uses it to bring dead souls back to life for His glory. For this reason, it is crucial that your congregation help this resident grow as a preacher.[5]

The Preaching Cohort will meet once a month for an hour to an hour and a half and will allow your resident to preach in a context where they will be given honest and helpful feedback from others. Along with the pastor, I would recommend inviting different leaders, as well as members of the congregation to come listen to the resident preach each month. Each observer will fill out a preaching evaluation sheet for giving critique in areas of strength and areas for growth.

The resident will preach a 25-30 minute sermon, followed by 15-20 minutes of evaluation and discussion. During this time, those present have the opportunity to offer words of encouragement and also share thoughts and observations that will help the resident identify areas for growth in their preaching. Always close this time by having those present spend time praying for him. For a sample preaching cohort evaluation, see **Appendix J**.

Putting It All Together: The Monthly Cohort Schedule

It is recommended that these three cohorts meet at the same time on the same day each week. For example, our church's residency cohorts meet from 4-6:00pm each Thursday afternoon at our church building. To get an idea of what the schedule for these cohorts looks like, see a sample of our fall schedule in **Appendix E**.

RESIDENCY COMPONENT #2: EXPLORE

Along with equipping the replanting resident, a second important residency component is helping the resident explore his vocational calling to church replanting and revitalization. It is important to connect the resident with a mentor who can pour into his life regularly during his time at your church. This will be a key relationship for the resident and will serve as a safe person who can encourage him, pray for him, and process with him over the course of the residency. This individual may be the pastor, an elder or deacon, or another mature lay leader in the congregation.

Steve Timmis speaks to the need for pastors and those preparing for ministry, such as replanting residents, to have a mentor, or shepherd, in their lives when he writes,

> Every shepherd in the church needs a shepherd. In the last 12 months, many pastors experienced trials and suffering. Some were health-related, others were family issues: major organ transplant, the rebellion of children, psychological damage of an adopted child, marital problems and adult children walking away from the

faith. These real issues devastated many of them for several months. Some pastor friends of mine dealt with their own cancer, loss of employment, abandonment by friends and betrayal by fellow elders, and others experienced serious financial setbacks. The pain is acute and in many cases, ongoing. I'm also aware of four suicides by pastors this last year. This is four suicides too many. The devastation on their churches and their families continues to impact the body of Christ in a major way.

The church leader is not exempt from problems. Quite frankly, the supernatural spiritual attack on church leaders is enormous and relentless. Who is shepherding the shepherds? Where do church leaders find their pastoral care? For many church leaders, they have no idea where to find help. Yet, they feel lonely, abandoned, and vulnerable. They deeply desire relationships, but are not sure if they want to share their heart's deepest concerns with members of the body—even other leaders, so they suffer in silence and as a result are not able to properly shepherd the flock where they have been assigned to oversee. The whole church suffers when the leaders suffer.[6]

Timmis' wise words iterate why we want to make sure we are doing a good job of preparing this replanting resident, not only for replanting a dying church, but for a healthy physical, spiritual, emotional, and relational life. As a result, it is important to pair up each replanter with a Resident C.O.A.C.H. There are five basic purposes and functions for a C.O.A.C.H.

Five Functions of a Resident C.O.A.C.H[7]

1. Comes alongside the replanting resident as a friend, mentor, and encourager.

2. Observes the life and ministry of the replanting resident carefully, offering feedback and critique as needed.

3. Asks questions of the replanting resident, his life, his family, and his ministry, wisely and helpfully.

4. Communicates potential growth strategies, along with resources, for the life and ministry of the replanting resident.

5. Holds accountable and cares for the heart of the replanting resident.

It will be important for the C.O.A.C.H. and the resident to go over these five functions together to help set expectations for the relationship before it begins. It is recommended that the C.O.A.C.H. and resident meet every other week for 1-2 hours each meeting. The more time spent together, the easier it will be to build trust with one another, which is vital to this type of coaching relationship.

Pairing the resident with a C.O.A.C.H. who they can share their joys, fears, hopes, and concerns with, will be of great benefit to their growth in life and pastoral ministry. Over the course of the year, this C.O.A.C.H. will help the resident honestly evaluate and explore their vocational calling to church replanting in a way that will hopefully bring greater conviction and clarity regarding God's direction for their ministry future. To help you discover more about being a mentor or coach, I recommend checking out these resources:

Mentoring Resources

Gospel Coach: Shepherding Leaders to Glorify God, Scott Thomas

Mentor Like Jesus: His Radical Approach to Building the Church, Regi Campbell

As Iron Sharpens Iron: Building Character in a Mentoring Relationship, Howard Hendricks and William Hendricks

Mentoring Millennials: Shaping the Next Generation, Daniel Egeler

Mentoring Leaders: Wisdom for Developing Character, Calling, and Competency, Carson Pue

The Heart of Mentoring: Ten Proven Principles for Developing People to Their Fullest Potential, David Stoddard

RESIDENCY COMPONENT #3: ENGAGE

Lastly, each replanting resident will spend significant time serving in various roles of ministry leadership within your church. This will help them to gain needed experience in multiple areas, which will help prepare them for future pastoral leadership in a replanting context. As a result, your church should intentionally seek out ways the resident can be involved on some level with the following ministries of your church:

- Youth and Children's Ministry
- Counseling and Pastoral Care
- Small Groups
- Worship Service Planning and Leadership
- Operations and Administration
- Local and Global Missions

- Assimilation and First Impressions
- Preaching
- Communications and Media

Providing opportunities for your resident to engage in these various ministry areas will not only be beneficial to the resident, but it will be beneficial to your congregation. For replanting residents who are married, be mindful and intentional about ways in which you can involve their wife in these areas of ministry as well, for her own ministry growth and development. You want the couple to get the most out of their ministry experience at your church, so consider these words of counsel:

#1: Give your resident freedom to try and fail.

If you want your resident to grow and mature as a pastor and leader, he needs plenty of opportunity to try and fail. In other words, create a culture where he can attempt new programs or implement a few new initiatives in your church. If they succeed, great! If they fail, extend grace. This is a learning experience. People come alive when they are allowed to dream without the fear of getting in trouble by leaders in the church. Before your resident goes out on his own to lead a Replant, let your church be soft ground for him to learn, grow, and fail, knowing your congregation is behind him 110%.

#2: Saturate your resident and his family with love and encouragement.

In Mark 12, Jesus tells us what the most important thing in the world is: Loving God with all your heart, soul, mind and strength and loving your neighbor as yourself. Love is to be the defining mark not only of our lives, but the defining mark of leadership development in our churches. This means we need to love and encourage our residents like crazy during this training process. Encouragement is so important. If you want to keep people fired up, encourage them! If you want your resident and his wife to be excited and energized in their time with your congregation, put a high priority on loving and encouraging them!

In Hebrews 3:13 we read, "But encourage one another daily, as long as it is called 'today' so that none of you may be hardened by sin's deceitfulness." Paul writes in 1 Thessalonians 5:11, "Therefore encourage one another and build one another up, just as you are doing." I believe the strongest form of motivation for many pastors and leaders in the church is loving encouragement. Encouragement is love spoken. It's that simple: love spoken. Your resident and his wife need a lot of it. Saturate them with love and encouragement.

#3: Give personal, specific, grace-filled, continual feedback.

Feedback is essential to one's growth in any area of life. It is especially important when raising up and developing pastors in the local church. Feedback is critical. But what kind of feedback is most helpful? There are four components to feedback that is both sharpening and encouraging to a resident. Feedback should be personal, specific, grace-filled, and continual.

First, it is personal. This means it is "in person." It is one-on-one and face-to-face. They can see you and hear you. The best feedback happens in relationship.

Second, it is specific. When you're giving feedback, don't be vague. Be clear and use specific examples. The best encouragement and the best critique is always detailed enough to be helpful while general feedback is typically unhelpful. For example, don't just say, "You did a great job preaching that sermon this morning!" Instead say something like, "I loved the way you applied your sermon to our lives this morning. The challenge you gave us to intentionally share a word of encouragement with each of our children before we put them to bed each night was so helpful. I am excited to put that into practice!" Be specific in your feedback.

Third, it is grace-filled. Intentional words of love and encouragement are what is going to earn you the right to have hard conversations with your resident. Grace-filled feedback creates a sense of safety and genuine care for them. Because you need to be specific, tempering that feedback with grace will protect the relationship with your resident.

Fourth, it is continual. Don't be the church that only gives intentional encouragement or has the hard conversations with a resident at the year-end review. Do it continually. Give thoughtful feedback on a regular basis in the context of your on-going relationship. This is how your church will help your resident grow the most.

The Two Evaluations

Though feedback should be given to the resident throughout the residency process, it is recommended that the resident participate in two evaluations over the course of the nine to twelve months they are with your church. All residents will receive an evaluation at the four to six month (halfway) point. This is designed to help steer the second half of the residency. Near the end of the residency, there will be a second evaluation to help provide direction for the resident's next steps after finishing the residency. Ideally, these evaluations will be conducted by the pastor and a few other leaders in the church, along with a denominational leader. Particularly in the second evaluation, a denominational leader can be of help in assisting your church and this resident determine next steps for their family, whether it be replanting a congregation or getting further training or education before launching into a replanting context.

It should be made clear from the beginning of the residency that the replanting resident is not guaranteed the endorsement of your congregation to replant a church. However, pending the results of the two evaluations, the hope is that this resident will be endorsed and directed in the next steps towards becoming a Lead Church Replanter with your church serving as the sending church.

Your church can do this!

Raising up replanters in the local church is needed and necessary and the time is now. Churches just like yours are beginning to join in this movement of replanting dying churches for the glory of God. Will you join them? My hope and prayer is that you and your church will join this movement of God! With more churches closing each week than at any other time in the history of the United States, the time for talking is over and the body of Christ must move to action. There is an urgency in this movement. At the same time, there is great hope and great joy! God is on the move and He is not done with dying churches. While your church has not been called to do everything to turn the tide of declining churches in our cities and communities, you have been invited by the Lord to *do something*. I pray that something might be the raising up and sending out of a replanter from your congregation. Your church can do this!

I pray you and your church will trust our Sovereign God, take a leap of faith, and invest in the preparation of a replanter for a season. Your church will be blessed, the Lord will be honored, and a church that is currently nearing its death may see a day of revitalization and transformation they can only dream of at this very moment... All because you chose to raise up a replanter.

APPENDICES

Appendix A

FREQUENTLY ASKED QUESTIONS

The following are several frequently asked questions regarding specific aspects of the replanting residency.

WHERE DO WE FIND A RESIDENT?

While at first it may seem daunting to find a replanting resident to come and serve in your church, it is not nearly as difficult as you might think. First of all, contact your area denominational leaders. Many times, these leaders are connected to all types of teachers, pastors, and leaders around the country. If nothing else, they can probably give you some contacts of other denominational leaders who might be connected with men desiring to pursue church replanting.

Secondly, reach out to your denominational seminaries. Increasingly, there are more and more theological students studying church revitalization. For example, in my own denomination (SBC), several of our seminaries have entire masters and doctoral programs devoted to church revitalization. These seminaries can be a gold mine when it comes to finding a potential replanting resident.

Thirdly, contact other pastors and churches that are passionate about revitalization and replanting. Many times these congregations have men who are considering going into replanting. This can be a way for your churches to partner if they are willing to send your church a resident to be trained under your care.

HOW MUCH DO WE NEED TO PAY A RESIDENT? WHAT ABOUT HOUSING?

As far as payment, the spectrum is very wide. It depends on the church and their financial situation. There are some congregations that bring residents on as full-time staff for the year they are with them. These congregations provide housing and a full-time salary for the resident and his family. Other churches are able to provide housing for the resident, but are unable to offer any salary. Still other congregations can offer in the ball park of $500-$1000 a month, but cannot help to pay for housing. However, most churches that choose to pursue this type of residency are unable to provide any money or housing.

Let me say that again: *most churches are unable to provide any money or housing for a resident.* I share this to show you that pursuing a replanting residency is not dependent on the financial package your church can put together. Most churches are just trying to pay their bills and make sure their pastor gets a pay check each month. They don't have extra cash to pay for a resident. That is okay. Money should not be the thing that makes or breaks your church's pursuit of a resident.

Keep in mind the resident is needing and desiring experience and mentoring in a local church. That is the greatest payment you can give them. Churches that are unable to pay a resident can also help in other ways such as helping the resident and his wife find a job, keeping a lookout for reasonably priced housing, or providing free babysitting for the family. There are all kinds of ways your church can serve this family without it costing a dime.

SHOULD THE RESIDENT BE AFFILIATED WITH OUR DENOMINATION?

Not necessarily. However, the reality is that when it comes to replanting dying churches, those dying churches most likely belong to a denomination and will be seeking a replanting pastor from that particular denomination. As a result, it typically makes the most sense for your church to find a resident that is part of your denomination or could become part of your denomination. This will allow for more doors to open when the time comes to seek out a church you want to help replant.

HOW MUCH SCHOOLING MUST THE RESIDENT HAVE BEFORE COMING TO OUR CHURCH?

There is no hard and fast rule here. I personally think it is helpful if the resident has finished or is finishing their formal theological training. A resident who has graduated from seminary and can now spend a year as a resident at your church before moving on to lead a church replant is ideal. Of course, there are situations where a resident has not yet been to seminary but because of life and ministry experience is seasoned and ready to pursue replanting. Again, there is not a hard line on this one. The key is making sure, as best you can, that the resident you bring on has the spiritual and emotional maturity to potentially replant a dying congregation once they finish their residency with you.

DO WE NEED TO CREATE A JOB DESCRIPTION FOR THE RESIDENT?

Yes. It is very important to be as clear as possible with the resident regarding expectations and responsibilities. If it is helpful, I've provided a sample job description in **Appendix C** that you can edit and use as you see fit.

Appendix B

RESIDENCY APPLICATION

Thank you for your interest in our revitalization and replanting residency program at Calvary Church. Our hope and prayer for this residency program is to encourage, educate, equip and unleash future pastors to lead revitalization in dying and declining churches for the glory of God. Under supervision, residents will gain knowledge and experience in the areas of pastoral leadership, shepherding, and preaching for a church revitalization context. We are excited about the possibility of you joining us!

There are 3 main parts to this application process. Please send each of the following via email to both mark@thecalvary.org and jeff@thecalvary.org:

1. An updated resume.
2. Two letters of recommendation (one from a current or former pastor).
3. The included application

The recommendation letters should speak to your character, experience, and skills, and should discuss both strengths and weaknesses. Please ask your references to state how long and in what relational capacity they have known you. If you are married, one of your two recommendation letters should be a letter from a pastor who can describe your marriage and speak to its suitability for ministry.

Please type and email the following application:

General Information

Name _____

Date of Application _____

Preferred Address _____

_____

Preferred Phone _____

Alternate Phone_____

Email address _____

Marital Status: Single/Married

Name of spouse _____

How did you hear about the Residency Program?

Educational Background

Please list all schools attended and both degrees started and degrees completed (high school, technical college, university, graduate school, Bible institute or seminary

Theological Alignment

Calvary Church joyfully partners in ministry and mission with both Acts 29 and the Southern Baptist Convention. Please read through the following doctrinal and philosophical statements for these two networks. Please share any areas of disagreement you have and why.

- **Acts 29 Overview** (Please read through this entire page) http://www.acts29.com/about/
- **SBC Baptist Faith & Message** http://www.sbc.net/bfm2000/bfm2000.asp

Strengths & Skills

- How would your friends and family describe you?
- List your top three strengths and top three areas of needed and desired growth:

Strengths:

1. _____
2. _____
3. _____

Areas of needed and desired growth:

1. _____

2. _____

3. _____

Personal Story

- What do you like to do for fun?

- What kind of music do you like? Favorite bands or artists?

- What are some of your favorite blogs or web-sites?

- What books have had the greatest impact on your life and why (other than the Bible)?

Please answer the following questions in 2-3 paragraphs:

- Please describe your faith journey. Include how God got your attention and some significant experiences and people that He used. How has this journey prepared you for this position?

- How has your past ministry experiences helped prepare you for this position?

- How does this position fit into your short and long-term goals? What do you hope to gain from this experience? Why do you want to do this?

Appendix C

RESIDENCY JOB DESCRIPTION

DESCRIPTION

The Calvary Family of Churches' Church Replanting Residency is designed to help church replanting residents explore their vocational calling, be equipped for pastoral ministry, be exposed to church replanting, and engage in missional living.

The residency is a twelve-month program, beginning in September and ending in August of the following year.

The residency consists of 3 distinct experiences: pastoral cohort (1st Thursday of the month, 4-6:00 PM), preaching cohort (3rd Thursday of the month, 4-6:00 PM), and the church replanting cohort (2nd and 4th Thursdays of the month, 4-6:00 PM). All residents will receive a mid-course evaluation, designed to help steer the second half of the residency and provide direction for the resident post residency.

EXPECTATIONS

Replanting residents will be expected to live and serve in a manner worthy of the Gospel (Phil. 1:27), by God's grace, seeking to love God with all they are, love others sacrificially, and make joyful, passionate disciples of Jesus (Matt. 22:37-39; 28:18-20).

Church replanting residents will be expected to give 8-10 hours a week to their cohorts and supervised ministry and an additional 5-8 hours a week to their homework and living on mission. Each week, residents will be expected to attend the scheduled cohort meetings, complete all required homework, and engage in all required ministry/mission experiences. Residents will also be expected to engage in a supervised ministry experience, which will be defined and determined by the local elders at Calvary Church Englewood.

EVALUATION

All replanting residents will participate in an evaluation, where the Calvary Family of Churches Church Replanting Director and 1-2 local elders from Calvary Church Englewood will work in concert with The North American Mission Board to assess the resident's progress and work with the resident to chart a course for the remainder of the residency and beyond. No Calvary Church replanting resident is guaranteed the endorsement of The Calvary Family of Churches to replant a church. However, pending the results of the evaluation, some residents will be endorsed and will be directed in next steps towards becoming a Lead Church Replanter.

Appendix D

RESIDENCY SYLLABUS

1. ATTENDANCE AND PARTICIPATION

Because presence is crucial to the work of church revitalization, residents are expected to be at all cohort meetings (1st and 3rd Thursdays: 4-6:00pm, 2nd and 4th Thursdays: 4-6pm on Thursdays, 5th Thursdays: OFF) and special events. They will also be required to attend Monday evening Shepherding meetings (5-6:30) and Wednesday afternoon staff meetings (2-3:30), unless other arrangements have been discussed and agreed upon.

2. READING REPORT

Each required text should be read reflectively, particularly focusing on how the material relates to the work of church replanting and revitalization. Residents will be required to complete four books per semester and submit a 2-3 page reading report for each. All four reading reports will be due by the end of the semester.

3. REPLANT ROUNDTABLES

Residents will participate in roundtable discussions of assigned readings and other material/special assignments. There will also be periodic roundtable discussions with successful church replanting and revitalization pastors. These will take place once a month on a Monday evening from 7:30-9:00pm at Calvary.

4. JOURNALING

Residents will keep a journal throughout the residency. The expectation is that the resident will journal 1-2 pages each week. These journals should reflect the soul work the student is doing, and reflect on how lessons learned through the readings and discussions can be practically applied in a local church context.

5. DECLINING CHURCH VISIT

One of the special assignments is for residents to go spend a morning visiting a congregation that is declining and in need of revitalization. The purpose of this visit will be to go encourage the folks who are there, taking part in whatever activities they have going on that day (probably a worship service and Sunday School class) and observe EVERYTHING that is going on…from the moment the resident steps out of your car to the moment they get back in to leave.

Residents will then write up a 3-5 page paper describing the experience. Be sure to include practical takeaways that can be applied to a future revitalization or replant ministry opportunity.

6. PASTORAL CARE/SHEPHERDING OBSERVATION OPPORTUNITIES

Residents will have some opportunity to observe and be part of pastoral care in action (Hospital Visits, Shepherding Visits, etc.) These opportunities will also arise through involvement in a Community Group. Residents should report on these opportunities in their Journal.

7. PRAYER

Because the work of a replanting pastor depends so much on the care for his flock, residents will be expected to pray systematically for the members of Calvary as part of their weekly shepherding responsibilities.

Appendix E

RESIDENCY SAMPLE SCHEDULE

REQUIRED READING

Christ-Centered Preaching, Bryan Chapell
Reclaiming Glory, Mark Clifton
Humility, C.J. Mahaney
The Shepherd Leader, Timothy Z. Witmer

NOTE: All reading assignments are due by the end of the stated month with the exception of Witmer's book. Have the Witmer chapters read and ready to be discussed for the Pastoral Cohort on the first Thursday of each month.

SCHEDULE (FALL 2016)

SEPTEMBER

2nd:   Pastoral Cohort #1
9th:   Preparing for Revitalization Pt. 1
16th: Preaching Cohort #1
23rd: Preparing for Revitalization Pt. 2
30th: NO MEETING

Reading:
-   Chapell – Chapters 1-2
-   Clifton – Chapters 1-2
-   Mahaney – Chapters 1-3
-   Witmer – Chapters 1-5 (finish for pastoral cohort)

OCTOBER

6th:   Pastoral Cohort #2
13th: Preparing for Revitalization Pt. 3
20th: Preaching Cohort #2
27th: The Heart of Revitalization Pt. 1

Reading:
-   Chapell – Chapters 3-5
-   Clifton – Chapters 3-5
-   Mahaney – Chapters 4-6
-   Witmer – Chapters 6-7 (finish for pastoral cohort)

NOVEMBER

3rd: Pastoral Cohort #3
10th: The Heart of Revitalization Pt. 2
17th: Preaching Cohort #3
24th: NO COHORT - Thanksgiving

Reading:
-   Chapell – Chapters 6-8
-   Clifton – Chapters 6-8
-   Mahaney – Chapters 7-9
-   Witmer – Chapters 8-9 (finish for pastoral cohort)

DECEMBER

1st: Pastoral Cohort #4
8th: The Heart of Revitalization Pt. 3
15th: Preaching Cohort #4

Reading:
-   Chapell – Chapters 9-11
-   Clifton – Chapters 9-10
-   Mahaney – Chapters 10-12
-   Witmer (Have finished by Pastoral Cohort) – Chapters 10-11

REPLANT ROUNDTABLES (2016- 2017)

(Mondays, 7:30-9:00pm, at Calvary)

2016

- September 26th
- October 24th
- November 14th
- December 12th

2017

- January 23rd
- February 20th
- March 20th, 2017 (Declining Church Paper Due)
- April 24th
- May 22nd
- June 26th
- July – OFF
- August 28th

Appendix F

COHORT SCHEDULE

CORE COMPONENTS

Opening & Session Overview (5 minutes): Welcome, Direct the Cohort Members to the desired objectives and outcomes for this session, Prayer.

Instruction (25-30 minutes): Together watch the teaching video of the particular Foundation(s) for the session. If the Cohort Leader would rather teach the Foundation(s) themselves (not using the video) they can use the provided Teacher's notes during this time. *NOTE: The actual instructional time should take roughly 30 minutes per Foundation being taught.*

Quick Debrief (10 minutes): The Cohort Leader will lead the Cohort in an initial discussion of key insights gained from the teaching/instruction time. (List on flip-chart or whiteboard).

Discuss & Develop (30 minutes): Guide Cohort through the discussion questions and exercises to stimulate thinking and work toward application.

Wrap Up (5 minutes): Review the key insights of this session and announce any assignments for the next gathering, pray and dismiss.

TIME ALLOTMENT

The time of each session will be directly related to the number of Foundations being taught and discussed. *Leaders should plan for roughly 1-1½ hours of instruction and discussion per Foundation.* The material can be used as a weekly gathering focused on one Foundation (1-1½ hour session), a bi-weekly gathering focused on two Foundations (2-3 hour session), or it can be used in a monthly cohort gathering format (4-6 hour session). Have the facilitator schedule in breaks as needed.

Appendix G

COHORT TOPICS
(40 Foundations)

PART 1: PREPARING FOR BIBLICAL REVITALIZATION
(September – October)

1. What is church revitalization?
2. Why is church revitalization needed?
3. Understanding God's heart for revitalization
4. Counting the Cost: Potential Disadvantages and Challenges in Revitalization
5. Counting the Joy: Potential Advantages and Opportunities in Church Revitalization
6. Is this church ready for revitalization?
7. Am I ready for revitalization?

PART 2: THE HEART OF BIBLICAL REVITALIZATION
(November – December)

8. Heart Posture #1: Humility
9. Heart Posture #2: Love

30. Showing and Telling the Gospel through Strategic Relational Evangelism
31. Redeeming Empty Space: Maximizing the Use of Your Church Building

PART 5: PERSEVERING IN BIBLICAL REVITALIZATION
(June & August)

32. Rooting Your Life and Ministry in The Gospel
33. Cultivating a heart for long haul ministry
34. Putting your Marriage and Family First
35. Growing in Emotional Intelligence
36. Facing Criticism in a Godly Manner
37. Handling Conflict Biblically
38. Caring for Your Soul through Spiritual Disciplines – resting well---- Bible and prayer
39. Managing Your Schedule
40. Training Up and Sending Out Church Revitalizers and Replanters

Appendix H

ADDITIONAL GROWTH OPPORTUNITIES

Beyond the learning that happens in the cohort groups, as well as through serving in various capacities within the church, I would recommend offering some extra, special growth opportunities for your resident throughout the year. The following are some of the extra growth opportunities we assign our residents:

READING REPORTS

Our expectation is that each required text is read reflectively, particularly focusing on how the material relates to the work of church replanting and revitalization. Residents are required to complete the assigned books for the semester and then submit a 2-3 page reading report for each book. All reading reports will be due by the end of the semester.

REPLANT ROUNDTABLES

These are roundtable discussions that take place once a month on a Monday evening from 7:30-9:00pm at our church. These roundtables serve as extra time to discuss assigned readings and other material/special assignments. Periodically we will use these roundtable discussions as an opportunity to meet or video-conference with successful church replanters around the country.

JOURNALING

Residents are expected to keep a journal throughout the residency. The hope is that the resident will journal 1-2 pages each week. These journals should reflect the soul work the student is doing, and reflect on how lessons learned through the readings and discussions can be practically applied in a local church context.

DECLINING CHURCH VISIT

One of the special assignments for our residents is to go spend a morning visiting a congregation that is declining and in need of revitalization. The purpose of this visit is to encourage the folks who are there, taking part in whatever activities they have going on that day (probably a worship service and Sunday School class) and observe *everything* that is going on from the moment the resident steps out of his car to the moment they get back in to leave. Residents then write up a 3-5 page paper describing the experience. We ask them to be sure to include practical takeaways that can be applied to a future revitalization or replant ministry opportunity. We spend one of our Replant Roundtables discussing these church visits.

Appendix I

FREE COHORT MATERIALS

In order to serve you and your church most effectively, we have launched a web-site where you can access free replant cohort materials for use in your own church as you start a replanting residency. Everything you need can be found at *nonignorable.org* or *churchreplanters.com*.

Specific to the replant cohort gathering, you can access all the teaching material for the 40 Foundations. Here you will find:

#1: VIDEO & AUDIO

Each of these "Foundation" teachings are between 20-30 minutes in length. These videos can serve as the primary teaching tool for your replant cohort group. If your pastor or another leader would prefer to teach rather than use the video teaching, the teaching notes are provided for each "Foundation". The audio Mp3's are available here as well.

#2: TEACHER'S NOTES

These are the main teaching outlines to use for each "Foundation." Again, leaders have the option of just watching the video teaching of this material, or they can use these outlines to teach the material themselves.

#3: STUDENT NOTES

These are the student notes that the resident and other cohort group members will receive for the teaching time. They have fill-in-the-blanks that will be filled in over the course of each teaching. You will notice that on the videos, the fill-ins come up on the screen. You can imagine that after the group concludes, the resident and other group members will have a very thick notebook of replant teaching material they can take with them for future use in their replanting context. The hope is this will be helpful material they can then share with other leaders wherever they go. *NOTE: I would recommend buying a binder for those involved in the cohort so they can compile their outline notes in one place.*

#4: DISCUSSION QUESTIONS

For each "Foundation"/Session we have written discussion questions that can be used for group interaction and reflection during each cohort gathering. These questions are at the end of both the teacher and student outlines.

Appendix J

PREACHING COHORT EVALUATION

Text:
Title:
Preacher:

When rating a sermon, use the following 1-5 scale: "1" means "not at all" or "poor", 3 means "consistently" or "fairly competent" and 5 means "always" or "extremely well done" Add additional comments below each set of numbers.

GENERAL

1. The speaker grabbed my attention. I found myself thinking, "I need to listen to this."

        1   2   3   4   5

2. The sermon held my interest throughout.

        1   2   3   4   5

3. The speaker seemed to be in awe of God and full of the Holy
   Spirit.

   1   2   3   4   5

4. The end of the sermon was compelling and moved me to action.

   1   2   3   4   5

DELIVERY

5. The speaker engaged the audience with himself through an
   appropriate use of humor and self-disclosure.

   1   2   3   4   5

6. There was a balance of warmth, love and humility on one hand
   and confidence, power and authority on the other.

   1   2   3   4   5

7. The speaker avoided any annoying mannerisms or phrases
   (sticking hands in pocket, saying "you know," self-conscious
   references, repeating themselves, nervous laughter).

   1   2   3   4   5

CONTENT

8. The preaching points were clearly rooted in the text.

   1   2   3   4   5

9. The flow of the sermon was concise, clear and easy to follow.

   1   2   3   4   5

10. The main idea/theme of the message was clear and persuasive.

     1   2   3   4   5

11. The sermon was the right length.

     1   2   3   4   5

APPLICATION

12. The speaker applied the text throughout – they didn't just explain the text; they helped me figure out how to apply it to my life.

     1   2   3   4   5

13. The sermon was gospel-centered: Christ and His finished work were applied as the solution to any problem.

     1   2   3   4   5

14. The sermon was evangelistic – it called non-Christians to repent and believe the gospel in a compelling way.

     1   2   3   4   5

15. The speaker avoided Christian jargon and statements that exclude non-Christians ("we all know the story…")

     1   2   3   4   5

16. The speaker engaged Christians, and showed how the gospel addresses their fears, hopes, problems, etc.

     1   2   3   4   5

FEEDBACK

Give top 2-3 strengths and 2-3 weaknesses. Be specific.

Appendix K

RECOMMENDED COHORT RESOURCES

PASTORAL COHORT

Leading with Love, Alexander Strauch
The Shepherd Leader, Timothy Witmer
Brothers, We Are Not Professionals, John Piper
The Reformed Pastor, Richard Baxter
Christian Ministry, Charles Bridges
Biblical Eldership, Alexander Strauch
Wisdom for Pastors, Curtis Thomas
On Being a Pastor, Derek Prime and Alistair Begg

REPLANTING COHORT

Can These Bones Live?, Bill Henard
Reclaiming Glory, Mark Clifton
The New Pastor's Handbook, Jason Helopoulos
The Conviction to Lead, Albert Mohler
Everyday Church, Tim Chester

Biblical Church Revitalization, Brian Croft
Humility, C.J. Mahaney
Comeback Churches, Ed Stetzer and Mike Dodson
The Advantage, Patrick Lencioni
Embers to a Flame, Harry L. Reeder, III
Church Planting is for Wimps, Mike McKinley

PREACHING COHORT

Expositional Preaching, David Helm
Christ-Centered Preaching, Bryan Chapell
Preaching, Timothy Keller
The Supremacy of God in Preaching, John Piper
Preaching for God's Glory, Alistair Begg
Saving Eutychus, Gary Millar and Phil Campbell
Preaching and Preachers, D. Martyn Lloyd-Jones
The Institute for Expository Preaching -   It is highly recommended, if possible, for your church to send your resident to "The Institute for Expository Preaching," sponsored by One Passion Ministries. I know of no other training available today that better equips a pastor for his biblical preaching ministry. Even if your resident has a seminary education, this training will be incredibly helpful and encouraging in his development as an expositor of God's Word. Go to onepassionministries.org for more information.

BIBLIOGRAPHY

"About." *Acts 29*. Accessed Mar 27, 2017. http://www.acts29.com/about/.

Baxter, Richard. *The Reformed Pastor*. New Edition. Banner of Truth Trust, Carlisle, PA: 1974.

Bridges, Charles. *Christian Ministry*. London: FB &c Ltd., 2015.

Begg, Alistair. Preaching for God's Glory. Redesign Edition. Wheaton, IL: Crossway, 2010.

Campbell, Regi. *Mentor Like Jesus: His Radical Approach to Building the Church*. Nashville: B & H Publishing Group, 2009.

Chapell, Bryan. *Christ-Centered Preaching: Redeeming the Expository Sermon*. Grand Rapids, MI: Baker Academic, 2005.

Chester, Tim. *Everyday Church: Gospel Communities on Mission*. Wheaton, IL: Crossway, 2012.

Clifton, Mark. *Reclaiming Glory: Revitalizing Dying Churches*. Nashville: B & H Books, 2016.

Croft, Brian. *Biblical Church Revitalization: Solutions for Dying & Divided Churches*. Fearn, Train, Scotland: Christian Focus Publications, 2016.

Egeler, Daniel. *Mentoring Millennials: Shaping the Next Generation*. Colorado Springs, CO: NavPress, 2003.

Helm, David. *Expositional Preaching: How We Speak God's Word Today*. Wheaton, IL: Crossway, 2014.

Helopoulos, Jason. *The New Pastor's Handbook: Help and Encouragement for the First Years of Ministry*. Grand Rapids: Baker Books, 2015.

Henard, William. *Can These Bones Live?: A Practical Guide to Church Revitalization*. Nashville: B & H Publishing Group, 2015.

Hendricks, Howard and William Hendricks. *As Iron Sharpens Iron: Building Character in a Mentoring Relationship*. Chicago: Moody Press, 1995.

Howard, Brian. "How to Develop Leaders in your Church." *Context Coaching*. Accessed January 23, 2017. http://contextcoaching.org/develop-leaders-church/.

Keller, Timothy. *Preaching: Communicating Faith in an Age of Skepticism*. New York: Penguin Books, 2016.

Lencioni, Patrick. *The Advantage: Why Organizational Health Trumps Everything Else In Business.* San Francisco: Jossy-Bass, 2012.

Lloyd-Jones, D. Martyn. *Preaching and Preachers*. 40th Anniversary Edition. Grand Rapids, MI: Zondervan, 2011.

Mahaney, C.J. *Humility*. Colorado Springs, CO: Multnomah Books, 2005.

McKinley, Mike. *Church Planting is for Wimps: How God Uses Messed-Up People to Plant Ordinary Churches That Do Extraordinary Things*. Wheaton, IL: Crossway, 2010.

Millar, Gary, and Phil Campbell. *Saving Eutychus: How to Preach God's Word and Keep People Awake*. Youngstown, OH: Matthias Media, 2013.

Mohler, Albert. *The Conviction to Lead: 25 Principles for Leadership That Matters.* Bloomington, MN: Bethany House Publishers, 2012.

Mohler, Albert. "Training Pastors in the Church." *Tabletalk Magazine*, February 1, 2008. Accessed March 18, 2017. http://www.ligonier.org/learn/articles/training-pastors-church/.

Ogne, Steve, and Tim Roehl. *TransforMissional Coaching*. Nashville: B&H Publishing Group, 2008.

Piper, John. *Brothers, We Are Not Professionals: A Plea to Pastors for Radical Ministry.* Updated and Expanded Edition. Nashville: B & H Publishing Group, 2013.

Piper, John. *The Supremacy of God in Preaching*. Revised and Expanded Edition. Grand Rapids, MI: Baker Books, 2015.

Prime, Derek, and Alistair Begg. *On Being a Pastor*. Revised and Expanded Edition of *Pastors & Teachers* © 1989. Chicago: Moody Publishers, 2004.

Pue, Carson. *Mentoring Leaders: Wisdom for Developing Character, Calling, and Competency*. Grand Rapids: Baker Books, 2005.

Reeder, Harry L., III. *Embers to a Flame: How God Can Revitalize Your Church*. Phillipsburg, NJ: P&R Publishing Company, 2004.

Stetzer, Ed, and Mike Dodson. *Comeback Churches: How 300 Churches Turned Around and Yours Can, Too*. Nashville: B & H Publishing Group, 2007.

Stoddard, David. *The Heart of Mentoring: Ten Proven Principles for Developing People to Their Fullest Potential*. Colorado Springs, CO: NavPress, 2009.

Strauch, Alexander. *Biblical Eldership: An Urgent Call to Restore Biblical Church Leadership*. Revised and Expanded Edition. Colorado Springs, CO: Lewis & Roth Publishers, 1995.

Strauch, Alexander. *Leading with Love*. Colorado Springs, CO: Lewis & Roth Publishers, 2006.

Thomas, Curtis. *Practical Wisdom for Pastors: Words of Encouragement and Counsel for a Lifetime of Ministry*. Wheaton, IL: 2001.

Thomas, Scott. *Gospel Coach: Shepherding Leaders to Glorify God*. Grand Rapids: Zondervan, 2012.

Timmis, Steve. "Every Shepherd needs a Shepherd." *Acts 29 Blog*. Accessed September 4, 2014. http://www.acts29network.org/acts-29-blog/every-shepherd-needs-a-shepherd/.

"The 2000 Baptist Faith & Message." *The Southern Baptist Convention*. Accessed Accessed Mar 27, 2017. http://www.sbc.net/bfm2000/bfm2000.asp.

Witmer, Timothy Z. *The Shepherd Leader*. Phillipsburg, NJ: P&R Publishing Company, 2010.

NOTES

[1] Brian Howard, "How to Develop Leaders in your Church," *Context Coaching*, accessed January 23, 2017, http://contextcoaching.org/develop-leaders-church/.

[2] Al Mohler, "Training Pastors in the Church," *Tabletalk Magazine*, February 1, 2008, accessed March 18, 2017, http://www.ligonier.org/learn/articles/training-pastors-church/.

[3] The time of each session will be directly related to the number of Foundations being taught and discussed. Leaders should plan for roughly 1-1 ½ hours of instruction and discussion per Foundation. The material can be used as a weekly gathering focused on one Foundation (1-1½ hour session), a bi-weekly gathering focused on two Foundations (2-3 hour session), or it can be used in a monthly cohort gathering format (4-6 hour session). Have the pastor or facilitator schedule in breaks as needed.

[4] See list of recommended book options in Appendix K.

[5] Beyond the monthly preaching cohort, it is highly recommended that your resident is given the chance to preach in the main worship gathering at least once every four to eight weeks. Preaching in a "real" worship service will not only help the resident continue to grow in confidence and skill as a preacher, but it will be a blessing to both the congregation and the Senior Pastor.

[6] Steve Timmis, "Every Shepherd needs a Shepherd," *Acts 29 Blog*, accessed September 4, 2014, http://www.acts29network.org/acts-29-blog/every-shepherd-needs-a-shepherd/.

[7] Adapted from Steve Ogne and Tim Roehl, *TransforMissional Coaching*, (Nashville, TN: B&H Publishing, 2008), 69-70.

the Replant Series

This series features short, action-oriented resources aimed at equipping the North American church for a movement of church replanting, introduced by Pastor Mark Hallock's book *Replant Roadmap*.

Thousands of churches are closing their doors in United States every year in some of its fastest-growing, most under-reached neighborhoods. Yet there is much hope for these churches, particularly through the biblically-rooted, gospel-saturated work of replanting.

Designed for both group and individual study, these books will help you understand what the Bible has to say about how God builds and strengthens his church and offer you some practical steps toward revitalization in your own.

For more information, visit **acomapress.org** and **nonignorable.org**

ACOMA PRESS

Acoma Press exists to make Jesus non-ignorable by equipping and encouraging churches through gospel-centered resources.

Toward this end, each purchase of an Acoma Press resource serves to catalyze disciple-making and to equip leaders in God's Church. In fact, a portion of your purchase goes directly to funding planting and replanting efforts in North America and beyond. To see more of our current resources, visit us at *acomapress.org*.

Thank you.

Made in the USA
Columbia, SC
26 April 2022